Baseball

Julie Murray

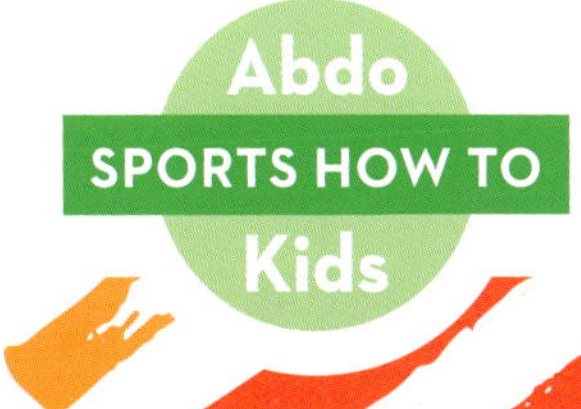

abdopublishing.com

Published by Abdo Kids, a division of ABDO, PO Box 398166, Minneapolis, Minnesota 55439.
Copyright © 2018 by Abdo Consulting Group, Inc. International copyrights reserved in all countries. No part of this book may be reproduced in any form without written permission from the publisher.
Printed in the United States of America, North Mankato, Minnesota.

102017

012018

THIS BOOK CONTAINS RECYCLED MATERIALS

Photo Credits: Alamy, Getty Images, Glow Images, iStock, Shutterstock

Production Contributors: Teddy Borth, Jennie Forsberg, Grace Hansen

Design Contributors: Christina Doffing, Candice Keimig, Dorothy Toth

Publisher's Cataloging in Publication Data

Names: Murray, Julie, author.

Title: Baseball / by Julie Murray.

Description: Minneapolis, Minnesota : Abdo Kids, 2018. | Series: Sports how to | Includes glossary, index and online resource (page 24).

Identifiers: LCCN 2017908183 | ISBN 9781532104114 (lib.bdg.) | ISBN 9781532105234 (ebook) | ISBN 9781532105791 (Read-to-me ebook)

Subjects: LCSH: Baseball--United States--History--Juvenile literature. | Baseball—Miscellanea --Juvenile literature.

Classification: DDC 796.357 --dc23

LC record available at https://lccn.loc.gov/2017908183

Table of Contents

Baseball

Sal loves baseball! He is ready to play.

baseball bat
helmet
jersey
batting glove
9

Baseball is played on a field.

There are 9 players on the field.

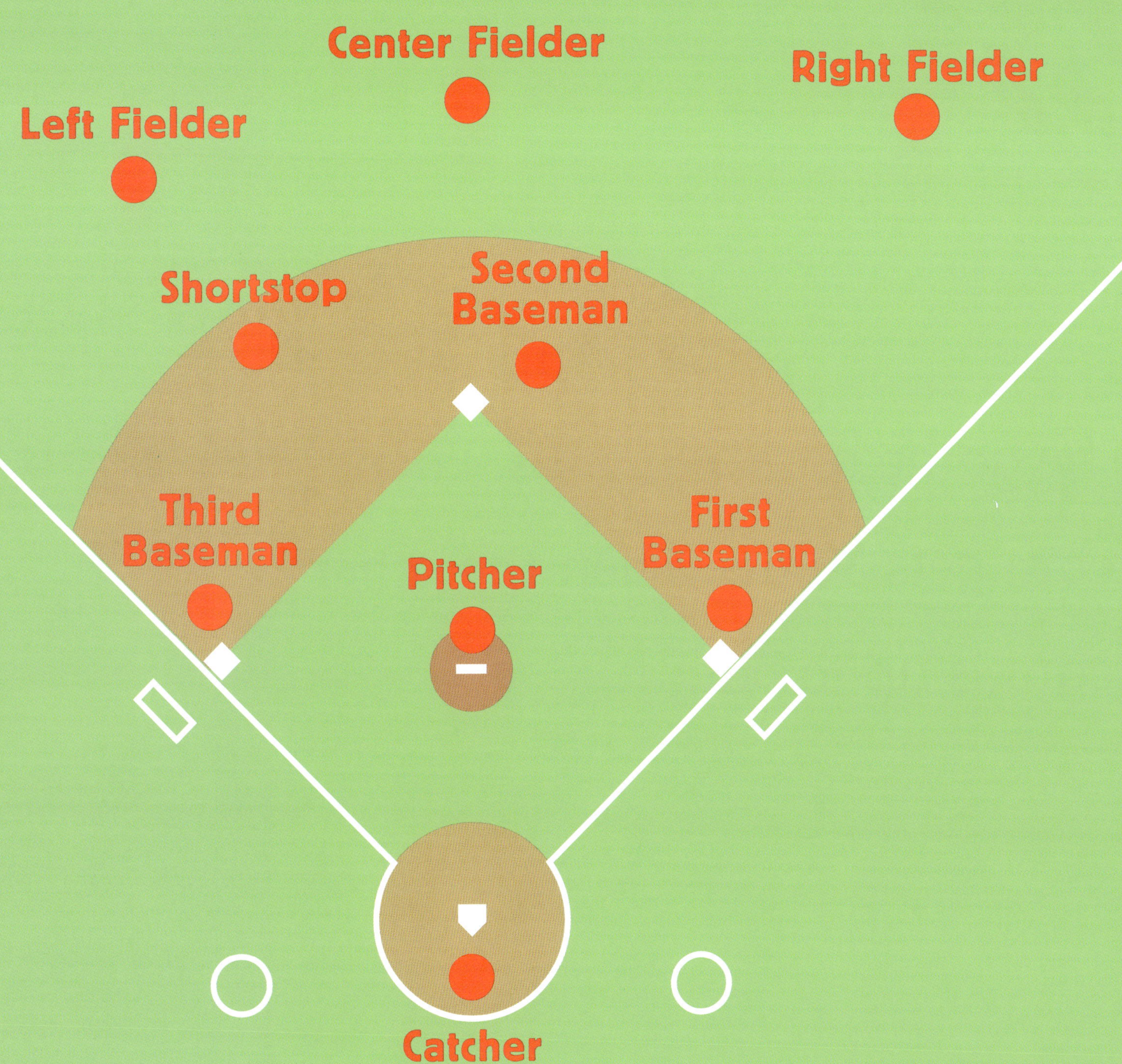
Center Fielder
Right Fielder
Left Fielder
Shortstop
Second Baseman
Third Baseman
First Baseman
Pitcher
Catcher

The game goes 9 **innings**. Each team gets 3 outs. Then the other team is up to bat.

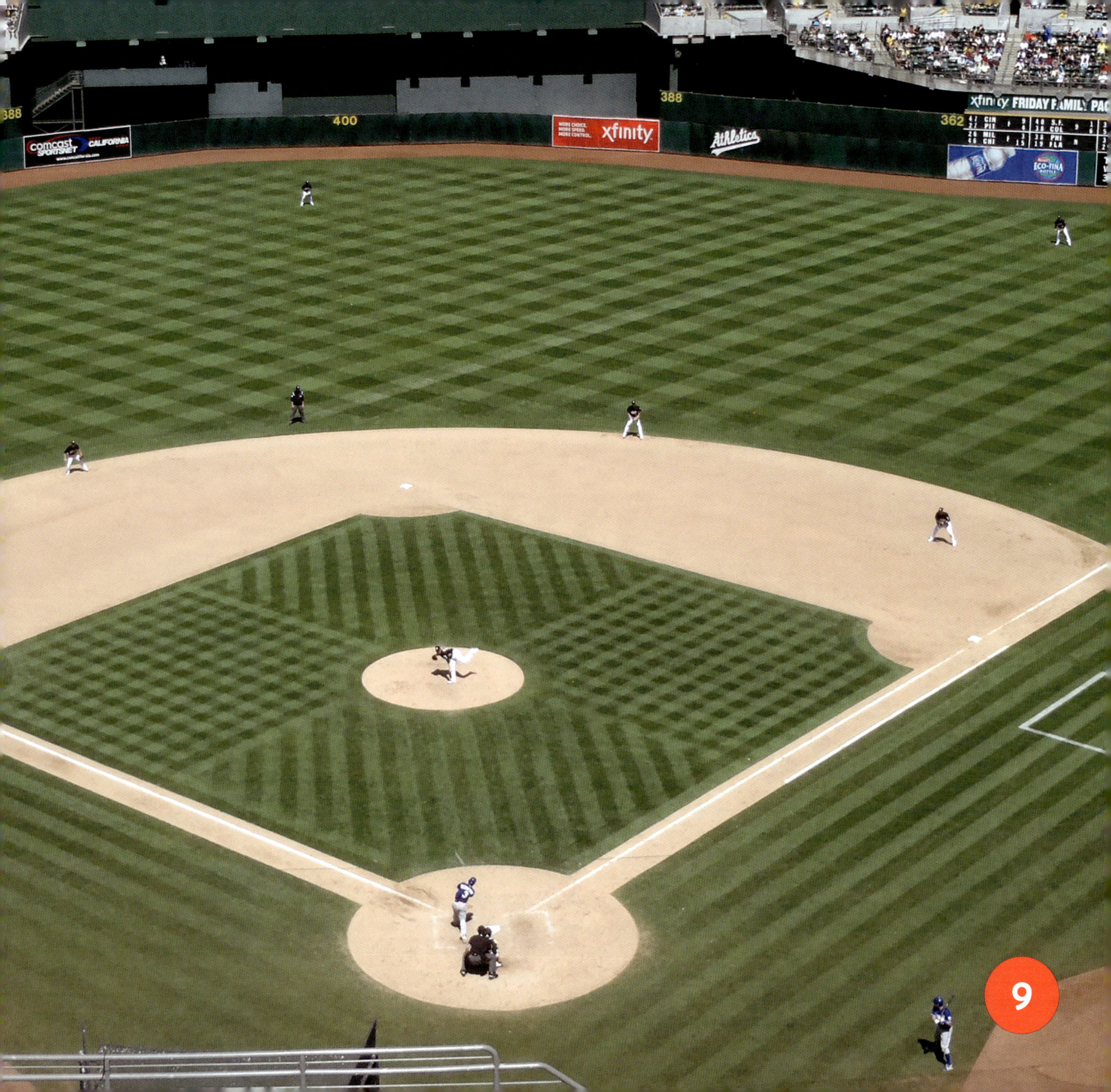
388
400
xfinity
Athletics
388
362
comcast SPORTSNET
CALIFORNIA

The pitcher throws the ball.

The batter tries to hit it.

3 **strikes** and Tim is out. 4 **balls** and he walks.

Brad is the catcher.

He wears special gear.

This keeps him safe.

Kay hits the ball. She runs to first base.

Todd is playing outfield. He catches the ball in his glove. That is an out!

Dan hits it over the fence.

Homerun!

Baseball Terms

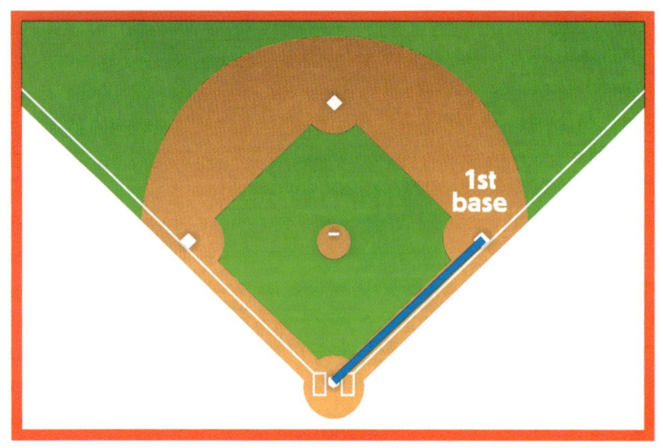

single

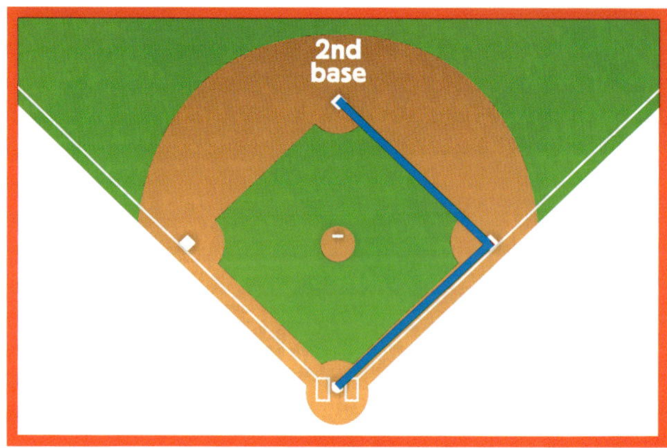

double

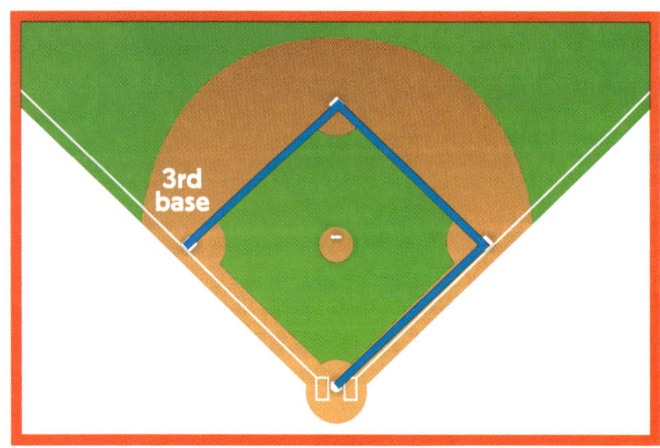

triple

homerun

Glossary

ball

a pitched ball that is not swung at by the batter and does not pass through the strike zone.

inning

time in a game when each team has a chance to score until they have three outs.

strike

a pitch that is swung at and missed by the batter.

Index

Visit **abdokids.com** and use this code to access crafts, games, videos, and more!